# I Love My Baby Sister

Written by Aaron and Jackie Boone
Illustrated by Mary Monette Barbaso-Crall

I LOVE MY BABY SISTER

Copyright 2013 Aaron and Jackie Boone

# DEDICATION

To our daughters Ana and Jessa.
We will love you always.

I have a baby sister and her name is Jessa.

I love my baby sister.

Every morning, I sneak into her bedroom and sit next to her, just watching her.

When she wakes up, I give her a good morning kiss.

She gives me a big smile.

Mommy gets Jessa up
and puts her in the exersaucer
in the living room so she can get breakfast ready.

When it's time for breakfast,
I pull my chair up next to her and we eat together.

After breakfast, I sing and dance in front of her and she watches me.

Sometimes mommy lets us
watch cartoons for a little while.

Sometimes we use mommy's pots and pans and play music together with a wooden spoon.

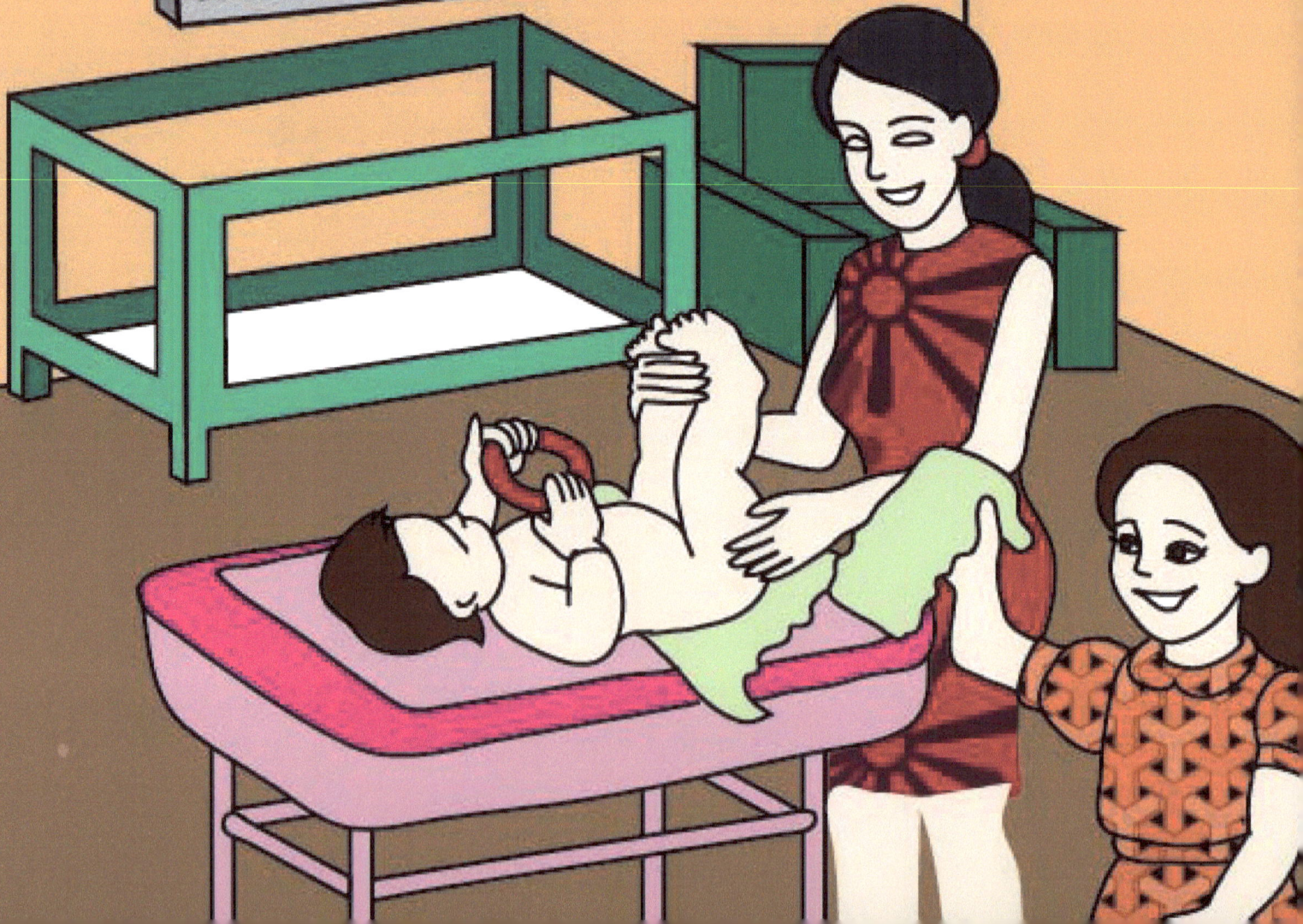

When it's time to change Jessa's diaper,
I help Mommy by getting the diaper
and giving her wipes.

For lunch, we have a picnic
on the kitchen floor
on a blanket with Mommy.

When it's time for Jessa's nap,
mommy lets me help get her milk ready.

I stay very quiet while
Mommy rocks Jessa to sleep.

After Jessa naps,
we play together on the floor
in the living room.

I roll a ball to her and she tries to roll it back to me.

I play peek-a-boo with her.

She likes to be tickled.

She likes to laugh at my jokes.

We pretend we're little bear cubs
inside a cave and Mommy
puts bear hats on our heads.

Then she takes a picture of us to show Daddy.

Sometimes when Jessa is crawling,
I pretend to have a crawling race with her.

I build a tunnel for us to crawl under.

At dinner time, I pull her high chair
next to me at the table
so we can eat next to each other.

Mommy lets me share some of my food with Jessa.

When Jessa takes a bath,
I bring her some of my bathtub toys and let her play.

She likes to splash the water all over the baby tub.

Jessa can't pick out her own clothes yet, so Mommy lets me choose pajamas for her.

Before bedtime, Daddy reads both of us a book.

When it's time to go to sleep,
I give Jessa a big goodnight kiss and a hug.
I tell her I love her.

I can't wait until my baby sister gets as big as me.

The End

Part of providing a happy and healthy environment for kids is helping them know what to expect when big changes, like welcoming a new baby to the family, are coming. This book is about the love siblings have for one another. Older siblings play a big role in their younger siblings' lives, as younger siblings always look up to them.

I Love My Baby Sister is a book that parents will enjoy reading to their young children because it teaches love and caring. It's also a tool for teaching older siblings about having a baby in the home.

www.ingramcontent.com/pod-product-compliance
Lightning Source LLC
Chambersburg PA
CBHW041221040426
42443CB00002B/42